STONE BENCH IN AN EMPTY PARK

Selected by Paul B. Janeczko
With photographs by Henri Silberman

Orchard Books   New York

For Karen Hutt,
my friend,
from Fenway Park
to Wrigley Field . . .
and beyond — P.B.J.

To Lyn, who helped make it possible — H.S.

Text copyright © 2000 by Paul B. Janeczko
Photographs copyright © 2000 by Henri Silberman

Page 40 constitutes an extension of the copyright page.

Orchard Books, A Grolier Company
95 Madison Avenue, New York, NY 10016

Manufactured in the United States of America
Printed and bound by Worzsalla Publishing Company
Book design by Mina Greenstein
The text of this book is set in 14 point Cochin.
The illustrations are black-and-white photographs printed in duotone.

10 9 8 7 6 5 4 3 2 1

Library of Congress Cataloging-in-Publication Data
Stone bench in an empty park / selected by Paul B. Janeczko ; with photographs
by Henri Silberman.   p.   cm.
Summary: An anthology of haiku accompanied by photographs reflect nature in the city.
ISBN 0-531-30259-8 (alk. paper) — ISBN 0-531-33259-4 (library : alk. paper)
1. City and town life — Juvenile poetry. 2. Children's poetry, American. 3. Nature —
Juvenile poetry. 4. Haiku, American. [1. City and town life — Poetry.
2. Nature — Poetry. 3. Haiku. 4. American poetry.] I. Janeczko, Paul B.
II. Silberman, Henri, ill.
PS595.C54 S76   2000   811'041080321732 21 — dc21   99-44282

Introduction

In Japan about nine hundred years ago, young poets gathered at parties to write a long collaborative poem called a *renga*. The most honored poet wrote the first short section of the renga; then each poet took his turn writing another short part. In the 1400s these short sections were freed from the long poem and eventually developed into haiku. Although haiku have been popular in Japan for centuries, they did not attract attention in Europe until the early part of this century. And it wasn't until the 1940s that Americans began to write haiku.

Generally speaking, a haiku will have these qualities:

- It contains seventeen syllables in lines of five, seven, and five syllables.
- It includes a word or two that alludes to the seasons.
- It usually has a theme of nature.
- It is written in the present tense about the present moment.

While these are the "rules" for writing haiku, you will notice that a number of the poems in this collection do not follow the rules. The writers of those haiku realize it is important to fulfill the spirit of the haiku rather than being slaves to syllable count and form. All the poets in this collection follow the advice of haiku master Daisetz T. Suzuki, who said that the haiku poet "gets inside an object, experiences the object's life, and feels its feelings." Because haiku are usually written about an image in nature, most of the haiku you have read probably described scenes in the country. But the city has its own wonderful scenes, and I gathered the poems for this collection because I wanted young writers to see that poetry and nature abound in the city as well as in the suburbs or country. We need to do what these haiku poets have done. We need to look carefully at what is around us. If we look closely enough, we will see poetry.

Paul B. Janeczko

A Note from the Photographer

I had been photographing the city for years when *Stone Bench in an Empty Park* presented me with a new challenge. Instead of letting my surroundings guide the subjects of my photographs, I let the haiku guide me. They already represented part of my view of nature in the city and contained unmistakable visual symbols: a seasonal event, a time of day, a sense of motion, a place or thing. I learned as I went along to look below the surface, and to use the process of photography to interpret the haiku. I shot a lot of film, looked at the images, then went back and shot some more until I found what I was looking for. Even though I planned many of the shots and chose the locations, these photographs are not always literal interpretations of the poems. It is often happenstance—the tilt of a girl's head or a shadow seen at the decisive moment—that made the photograph work.

Henri Silberman

STONE BENCH IN AN EMPTY PARK

The bridge toll-booth—
from the dark a hand collects
rain on the coins

David E. LeCount

in front of the newsstand
a spring wind
ripples the Sunday funnies

Cor van den Heuvel

Between tall buildings
a window of sky opens . . .
lets in the rain

Erica Silverman

driving
out of the car wash

clouds move
across the hood

Alan Pizzarelli

In the rains of spring
An umbrella and raincoat
Pass by, conversing

Buson

sudden shower
in the empty park
a swing still swinging

Margaret Chula

Pines, tamed by fences,
pop their heads over to look
out at the traffic . . .

Myra Cohn Livingston

Wild branches, spilling
over the concrete wall, reach
out to touch the bus . . .

Myra Cohn Livingston

Scarlet butterfly
posing on my handlebars
hitching a free ride.

Nikki Grimes

all night long
light shines in the eyes
of the carousel ponies

Penny Harter

Stickball players shout
as moonlight floods their field
from curb to curb

Paul B. Janeczko

Jumping double dutch
over the L.A. summer —
the Queen of the Hop.

J. Patrick Lewis

To benches, to grass,
offices fall out for lunch—
sunlight's on London!

James Berry

Ice-cream wrappers bloom
In overflowing baskets.
Summer in the park.

Jane Yolen

Three guys make my day—
rhythms on plastic paint pails—
each beat saying "Live!"

Bobbi Katz

from the tar papered
   tenement roof, pigeons
      hot-foot it into flight

Anita Wintz

Spring minus the rain:
City sidewalks purse gray lips.
No manholes gurgle.

Pigeons strut the rails
Of the city reservoir
Doing a rain dance.

Jane Yolen

One chrysanthemum
in a vase, watching over
Second Avenue

Myra Cohn Livingston

At the flower stand
Mama's Valentine rose waits
while I count my coins.

Nikki Grimes

Yellow long-necked beasts
munching clods of dirt . . .
giraffes or cranes?

Erica Silverman

All summer long
the sixteen-story crane
bows and bows

J. Patrick Lewis

Hard hat
   the yellow bud
      upon the forked stem.

Peter Neumeyer

Screeching and clawing
a trash truck drowns out the protests
from the alley cat

Paul B. Janeczko

full moon shining
squeezes between skyscrapers

f
l
u
o
r
e
s
c
e
n
t

Anita Wintz

Railroad tracks: a flight
of wild geese close above them
in the moonlit night.

Shiki

November evening—
the wind from a passing truck
ripples a roadside puddle.

Cor van den Heuvel

Between lace curtains
the white cat's eyes
follow a snowflake

Doris Heitmeyer

sun brightens
snow   slides off
the car bumper

Alan Pizzarelli

caught
     in the crooked icicles—
       the wind

Virginia Brady Young

my
house's
first
icicle
gray
with
soot

Issa

like
he's
biting
at
the cold
moon
gargoyle

Issa

the windy stars—
the distant gas station lights
go out

Cor van den Heuvel

Acknowledgments

Grateful acknowledgment is made to the following for permission to use material owned by them. Every reasonable effort has been made to clear the use of the poems in this volume. If notified of any omissions, the Publisher will make the necessary corrections in future editions.

"To benches, to grass" by James Berry from *Everywhere Faces Everywhere*, copyright © 1997 by James Berry. Reprinted with the permission of Simon & Schuster Books for Young Readers, an imprint of Simon & Schuster Children's Publishing Division.

"In the rains of spring" by Buson from *The Japanese Haiku*, edited by Kenneth Yasuda, copyright © 1957 by Kenneth Yasuda. Reprinted by permission of Charles E. Tuttle Co., Inc. of Boston, Massachusetts, and Tokyo, Japan.

"sudden shower" by Margaret Chula from *Grinding My Ink*, copyright © 1993 by Margaret Chula, Katsura Press. Reprinted by permission of the author.

"At the flower stand" and "Scarlet butterfly" by Nikki Grimes. Copyright © 1999 by Nikki Grimes. Reprinted by permission of the author.

"all night long" by Penny Harter from *Shadow Play*, published by Simon & Schuster, copyright © 1994 by Penny Harter. Reprinted by permission of the author.

"Between lace curtains" by Doris Heitmeyer from *Frogpond XI:1* (part of sequence, "Wintering Over") copyright © 1998 by Doris Heitmeyer. Reprinted by permission of the author.

"in front of the newsstand," "November evening," and "the windy stars" by Cor van den Heuvel from *Curbstone*, Chant Press, copyright © 1998 by Cor van den Heuvel. Reprinted by permission of the author.

"Like" and "my" by Issa from *Issa: Cup-of-Tea Poems*, translated by David G. Lanoue, copyright © 1991 by David G. Lanoue. Reprinted by permission of Asian Humanities Press.

"Screeching and clawing" and "Stickball players" by Paul B. Janeczko. Copyright © 2000 by Paul B. Janeczko. Reprinted by permission of the author.

"Three guys make my day" by Bobbi Katz. Copyright © 2000 by Bobbi Katz. Reprinted by permission of the author.

"The bridge toll-booth" by David LeCount from *Virtual Image 1/1*, copyright © 1982 by W. Elliot Greig. Reprinted by permission of the author.

"Jumping double dutch" and "All summer long" by J. Patrick Lewis. Copyright © 1998 by J. Patrick Lewis. Reprinted by permission of the author.

"One chrysanthemum," "Pines, tamed by fences," "Wild branches, spilling" by Myra Cohn Livingston from *Cricket Never Does*. Text copyright © 1997 by Myra Cohn Livingston. Reprinted with the permission of Margaret K. McElderry Books, an imprint of Simon & Schuster Children's Publishing Division.

"Hard hat" by Peter Neumeyer. Copyright © 2000 by Peter Neumeyer. Reprinted by permission of the author.

"driving" and "sun brightens" by Alan Pizzarelli from *Hike*, Islet Books. Copyright © 1984 by Alan Pizzarelli. Reprinted by permission of the author.

"Railroad tracks: a flight" by Shiki from *An Introduction to Haiku* by Harold G. Henderson, copyright © 1958 by Harold G. Henderson. Reprinted by permission of Bantam Doubleday Dell.

"Between tall buildings" and "Yellow long-necked beasts" by Erica Silverman from *Beasts, Sky*, copyright © 1999 by Erica Silverman. Reprinted by permission of the author.

"full moon shining" and "from the tar papered" by Anita Wintz. Copyright © 2000 by Anita Wintz. Used by permission of Marian Reiner for the author.

"Ice-cream wrappers bloom" and "Spring minus the rain" by Jane Yolen. Copyright © 1999 by Jane Yolen. Reprinted by permission of Curtis Brown, Ltd., and the author.

"caught" by Virginia Brady Young. Copyright © 2000 by Virginia Brady Young. Reprinted by permission of the author.